Fool Me Once:
Should I Take Back My Cheating Husband?

By Caroline Madden, MFT

TRAIN OF THOUGHT
PRESS

Publisher's Note

This book is designed to provide information and motivation to our readers. It is sold with the understanding that the publisher is not engaged to render any type of psychological, legal, or any other kind of professional advice. No warranties or guarantees are expressed or implied by the publisher's choice to include any of the content in this volume. No therapeutic relationship is established. Neither the publisher nor the individual author shall be liable for any physical, psychological, emotional, financial, or commercial damages, including, but not limited to, special, incidental, consequential, or other damages. Our views and rights are the same: You are responsible for your own choices, actions, and results.

ISBN: 978-0-9907728-5-9

Summary: Advice from a therapist if a woman should take back her cheating husband

Connie Johnston
Train of Thought Press
2275 Huntington Drive, #306
San Marino, CA 91108
Connie@TrainofThoughtPress.com
www.TrainOfThoughtPress.com

Table of Contents

Introduction

You've discovered that your husband has cheated on you. Maybe you've discovered incriminating emails or text messages from his lover, or, worse yet, have actually seen them together. Your world is crashing down. You feel like a nuclear bomb just decimated your entire world, and you are trying to shield yourself from the fallout. This is very likely the most painful experience you've ever had. You've been sucker punched in the soul.

You are so confused. Your emotions are volatile – one minute you're so angry you could claw his eyes out, the next moment you're devastated with grief because you fear he will leave you.

You never wanted a divorce, but somehow you are now in this position. Do you take him back or blow up your family? What about the kids? It's all so unfair!

Ever since you were a young woman, you told all your friends that if your man ever cheated on you, you would be so out of there. But life isn't black and white anymore, is it? You love your husband. Sure, there might have been issues, but you know that marriage is work.

You've built a life together. You have a home. You have children. You cringe at the idea of being a single mother and hitting the dating scene. You want to stay married. But then you think to yourself, "Only weak women stay with cheaters. Strong women walk!"

I'm here to tell you an affair doesn't mean it has to be over.

How do I know this? I work as an affair recovery specialist, serving as a Marriage and Family Therapist in California. I work almost exclusively with adults with significant relationship problems. Dealing with the aftermath of affairs is my specialty.

I'll tell you what <u>strong</u> women do. They sit back and let the dust settle. Right now, you are one of those snow globes you pick up as a souvenir when you travel. You are all shaken up, and you need to let some of those snowflakes settle to gain clarity as to what the picture is.

You may not realize it, but you are in a state of trauma right now, so you shouldn't be making any big decisions just yet. That includes putting your house up for sale, putting all his stuff in the street, calling the affair partner's husband, and/or telling everyone in the world that he cheated on you. When you regain your composure, these are all things you will regret. *Trust me.*

As a therapist, I help women like you determine if the man who has betrayed them should be trusted or not. In some cases, I help them decide if the relationship itself is worth saving, even if the unfaithful man seems sincerely repentant.

If you are like most women I see in your situation, you are thinking that there is no way your relationship can survive this explosion.

Believe it or not, statistics prove that many couples survive affairs. You probably feel like you will never be capable of trusting him again, and forgiveness may seem impossible right now. However, relationships do evolve and grow stronger if both parties are truly committed to working things out. I see it happen all the time.

Fool me once, shame on *you*. Fool me twice, shame on *me*.

Note what I said in that last paragraph: Relationships do evolve and grow stronger *if both* parties are truly committed to working things out.

I know you're probably very confused right now. Perhaps he seems genuinely sorry. He might be calling you, weeping, and begging you to let him move back in (or for you to come home, if you left). You may be so angry you never want to see him again, and you might fear what your friends and family will think if you give him a chance.

But here is the real question you are probably asking yourself:

"If I do let him come back, will he do this to me again?"

It's the old adage, "Fool me once, shame on *you*. Fool me twice, shame on *me*." You worry that you won't be able to forgive yourself for being so stupid. If other people know you took him back after he cheated, they will think you got what you deserved. If you take him back, he will just think you are a doormat and he can do it again. And frankly, you are not sure you can survive another affair. Just. Can't. Again.

Am I safe in taking him back or am I a complete idiot to trust him again?

In the decade that I have been treating couples, I've had an extremely high success rate in helping couples recover from affairs. How have I done this? I've learned how to identify why a man has cheated, if he sincerely wants to save the marriage, and what elements in the relationship need to change for the couple to make it out of the dungeon of despair.

I also screen out men that I have a gut feeling are one or more of the following: sexual addicts, philanderers, entitled jerks, and those with personality disorders. In this book, I have done my best to share with you the criteria I use when assessing a man to determine if he is truly remorseful and is determined not to cheat again. I hope you find this helpful as you make this very difficult decision.

Five Things That May Look Suspicious (But Probably Aren't)

The first thing I want to do is to tackle the things that look shady to a woman who has been cheated on but aren't necessarily indications that your husband is insincere.

He may be doing some things that make you question his sincerity and/or ability to recommit to you. Something to keep in mind is that your husband is a *man*. He is doing things that he thinks will help you through this but that are actually making the situation worse. No matter how sincere he is, there are some things he just isn't going to get.

The following are five actions that look shady but don't necessarily mean he isn't trying to get things right with you:

1. You keep finding out more details through the drip, drip, dripping of truth-telling.

Every time you think you have the whole story of the affair, you discover something new that he "forgot" to tell you. This can be incredibly upsetting, because this slow drip, drip, drip of the truth repeatedly undermines your ability to trust him.

I have seen a lot of women in my office who have actually divorced their husbands over this maddening method of confession – the slow leaking of information and confessions, or the telling of half-truths. This can wear on your patience and make it very difficult for you to repair the relationship and move forward.

You may think he is doing this because he doesn't want to be honest with you, but it's more likely that he is a coward than a man who wants to deceive you. He thinks he is being nice to you by not upsetting you with all the truth at one time.

This is how I often see this play out:

You catch him in his infidelity, maybe finding a text from his lover or an incriminating email.

You confront him, and he confesses that yes, he met up with her once, or slept with her a time or two, but he insists that's all it was.

He breaks up with her and recommits himself to you, and he thinks he is doing fine. After all, he's done with her and is committed to you.

However, you find more evidence about the affair, and you discover something that proves that he slept with her more than the once or twice he admitted took place. You're furious, so you confront him, and he admits to whatever you have discovered.

He continues to rebuild the relationship, and he feels confident everything will okay. He thinks it doesn't matter if you don't know how many times he slept with her or how long he had a crush on her.

You continue to find yet more information, like a love note he hasn't thrown away, dated from long before he admitted the affair started, and you confront him yet again. Once again, he admits it, and he keeps on chugging along like there's no problem.

Here's what happens in a situation like this. You feel like he has betrayed you by not admitting the full truth, and you worry what else you might discover. You fear that the whole truth will be too much for you to handle, and you anticipate the worst.

Your husband, on the other hand, is confused as to why you'd be so upset. He is afraid of telling you the whole truth all at once because he is afraid you won't be able to handle the pain. He is afraid you might leave him. He is hoping you'll never find out the whole truth because he truly regrets his choices and he just wants to recommit to you and move forward towards healing. He knows what is in his heart. He knows it's over. The details of the affair are just painful reminders to him of how stupid he was.

Another way this sometimes plays out: the confessor
Another common scenario is the one where the husband confesses little by little, saying, "I meant to tell you this that first time we talked about my affair, but I realized I forgot to tell you this..." Then BOOM! He shares something that slices open your heart again, reopening wounds that were just starting to heal.

A man like this feels guilty and wants to be forgiven. He was too afraid to come clean with everything upfront, and now he's trying to absolve his guilt by confessing in small chunks and asking for your forgiveness.

This puts you in a very bad position. You either have to be the "bad person" who won't forgive, or you have a brand new fight every time he confesses. A man like this is being selfish, but he may just be misguided and think he can't be close to you unless you know everything. This is probably because he can't stop thinking about the ways he has wronged you, and he feels like all this guilt is getting between you.

Of course, his true motivation is to avoid getting into any more trouble than he is in already. He doesn't understand that the drip, drip, drip of information makes you crazy and feel like you can't trust him.

What to do...
Tell him that you need him to come clean with everything, right now. No more bits and pieces of the truth over time. Tell him you have the right to know the whole truth and you can't handle this never-ending revealing of more painful information. Ask him to man up. Then ask for some time to think things over and to make your decision, once you know the whole truth and have had some time to process the situation.

2. He is upset that you are telling other people.
If you've told a lot of people what happened and your husband has asked you to please stop doing this, you may be very angry with him. After all, he had full knowledge of what was going on in your relationship, while you were operating with only some of the information. Now that you are processing the reality of what happened, you may feel the need to tell others and get support as you work through the pain and move forward.

You may think your husband isn't truly sorry or willing to recommit if he isn't willing to let you tell whomever you want to tell, but that probably isn't that case. It's more likely that he simply considers this quite embarrassing or is worried that the information will get back to the wrong people. He may be afraid of the following possible scenarios:

- The information will get back to your children, who may be forever scarred by the knowledge that their father cheated on their mother. You may think otherwise, but as an experienced therapist, I ask you to PLEASE not tell your children or anyone who might tell your children. Even adult children can be affected (deeply, negatively) by this sort of revelation, and it can affect their ability to love and trust a romantic partner. Your husband is right to want to protect the kids from this information.

- The information will get back to your family, who may not be able to forgive him if the two of you work it out. He may legitimately care that your family relationships stay strong and harmonious. This is also a valid concern. If you want to work it out with your husband, it is best if your family does not know about his infidelity, as many family members are unable to forgive.

- The information will get out to his affair partner's husband, who might do things that negatively impact your life. He could call your husband's work and get him fired or, worse, show up at your house with a gun and kill him. This is also a realistic and prudent concern. You might be tempted to tell his affair partner's

9

[handwritten margin note: jim dodged a bullet]

husband (if she is married), but you have to recognize the very real possibility that you will endanger your husband and even your family.

In most cases, it isn't that he doesn't want you to get support – it's that he doesn't want people to hate him and give him the evil eye every Thanksgiving for the rest of his life. Let's face it: You probably don't want this to happen, either.

What to do...

Only tell people you know can keep a secret and who will support the two of you if you do manage to repair the relationship. Do not tell people to shame him and to let the world know what a jerk he is. If you work this out with your husband, it will make every family gathering and every neighborhood BBQ painful for BOTH of you.

[handwritten margin note: That's true + those + are the only ones who know]

If you do not have anyone that you can trust to one, keep a secret, and/or two, accept your husband if you decide to stay with him, I strongly suggest you see a therapist individually as you work through this difficult time. A therapist is bound to confidentiality and will know what to say to give you constructive support.

3. When asked why he cheated, his answers sound like he is blaming you.

There is a difference between him trying to explain what happened to erode his commitment to you and a man blaming you for his bad choices. You will have to listen carefully to distinguish what the situation is.

You've probably asked him why he cheated, right? You genuinely want to know what he was thinking and what happened. Deep down, you also probably wonder if you did anything that contributed to the weakening of your emotional bond to the point where he was susceptible to temptation.

Put yourself in his position. If you had cheated, and your husband asked you why you did it, how would you answer him? Would ANY answer be sufficient?

You will never hear the right answer, because to you, no reason is good enough. But ask yourself, if he said it was because you never had sex (and he had previously told you this was a problem), did you still go months or even years without having sex? If he says you criticize him all the time, do you?

No, you aren't to blame for his choice to betray you, but my point is that in his mind, this is the reason why he strayed. He may just be trying to tell you what was going on with him that he made such a terrible decision to betray you.

Reasons are different than blame. (But no reason is good enough. I'm just explaining what he may be thinking.)

What to do...
Tell him if you are not ready to hear his "reasons" for cheating. You may need time to heal and see that he is truly committed to you before you can work on improving the marriage. However, if you don't want to hear his perspective on the marriage, you have to *stop*

11

asking him why he cheated. Don't ask why until you are ready to work together to repair the relationship.

To move forward, you will have to see the marriage and your actions through his viewpoint. It doesn't make his decision to cheat right, but at least you might understand better what the hell he was thinking.

Here is an analogy that might help:

You come home to find your house robbed. Your stuff is gone, but worse yet, your sense of safety has been stolen, too. You look around the house and you realize that the bathroom window had been left open and that is how the burglar got in.

Did you deserve to get robbed because you left the window open? No. But aren't you going to make sure it's locked the next time you leave the house?

Did you deserve to get cheated on because of (fill in his excuse here)? No. But shouldn't you find out what might have made your relationship vulnerable in his mind?

The answer is yes. When you are ready to handle it and work together to repair the relationship, you will want to know this information.

4. He makes a mistake.
It happens to every man during affair recovery, and almost every wife freaks out when it happens. This is the set-up:

He says he will be home at 5:00, but he doesn't get home until 5:30. In between 5:00 and 5:30, you can't reach him on the phone, and you, of course, freak out, thinking he is sleeping with his affair partner again. You have this whole awful scene playing through your head... His affair partner was waiting for him in the parking lot, and when he saw her, he was swept up by lust and love, and they drove somewhere secluded and did unspeakable things.

By the time he gets home, you are going ballistic, so he says it is nothing. He insists nothing happened and that you are overreacting.

This is the deal: He has no idea that your whole world has changed and that the secure wife who didn't keep tabs on him is now watching his every move. With any luck, he will learn from this and will not repeat the exact mistake again. He will probably do stupid things that, in your mind, defy common sense, but which he might think are completely rational.

What to do...
Explain to him why you got upset. Then let him know exactly what you need from him. Would it help if he put a "friend finder" tracking app on his phone so you always know where he is? Do you want him to text you if he's going to be late or something is taking longer than he anticipated? Determine what will help you feel secure, and let him know what you need.

5. He says, "I don't want to talk about it anymore" or "I don't want to answer the same questions over and over again."

13

This response can cut life a knife. First, he has lied to you, and now he is shutting you down and deciding for you (again) what you need to know and what you don't need to know.

What's happening in his mind: You *have* asked the same questions over and over. Whenever he answers you, it's not good enough and you just get more upset. He is doing his best to answer your questions, but nothing he says is ever good enough, and he doesn't know what to do when you get angry.

Also, he feels that you two are stuck and not moving forward. He might say something like, "I don't think this is helping you get past this."

Try not to kill him if he says this. He doesn't really mean, "Get over it, already." Most men are willing to answer whatever questions you have as long as they see that answering the questions helps and serves a purpose.

This is what is happening in his mind: He doesn't think talking about it is helping. He hopes not talking about it will help you move on.

He also feels that you are bringing the affair up out of the blue. He doesn't understand that you are triggered by every song on the radio and by every time he says he is doing something that he used to use as his alibi (even though you believe that he truly is just at the hardware store). He doesn't understand that every little thing triggers reminders that your marriage has been irrevocably altered, and because of this, he feels ambushed, and he doesn't know what to do.

He also worries that you don't actually want the answers to the questions you are asking. He thinks that you are just trying to trap him in a lie so you can yell at him. Let's be honest, you probably *are* trying to trap him in a lie. He is sick of playing the game; he wants to move forward. He wants to repair the marriage, even though you might not be ready to do that quite yet.

Conclusion: You will need to examine these areas carefully.

If your husband has been doing any of the five things I described above, he probably is trying to repair the relationship but is simply clueless about what you need from him. A good marriage counselor can help him make fewer mistakes and help you communicate what you need from him to enable you to feel safe again.

5 Signs You Should Give Him Another Chance

You're probably afraid that you will get hurt again – even worse – if you trust him again, take him back, and then he betrays you a second time. Then you will feel like a fool on top of all the pain you are already enduring.

I get this, and I want to help you determine if he is trustworthy so that you can make the choice that is truly best for you.

To that end, I would recommend that you first ask yourself if the relationship itself is worth saving.

When you think back on the relationship, was it mostly good? Loving? Nurturing? Mutually edifying?

If you didn't know about the affair, would you want the relationship to continue? Or were you thinking about ending the relationship anyway?

If you determine that the relationship itself is something you wish you could continue, and if you want to be with him (assuming you do someday manage to forgive him), then you'll want to watch for the following five signs.

The Five Signs That a Man is Truly Sorry and is Worthy of Your Trust

The five signs I'm going to describe for you are signs I've seen in men who are willing to completely recommit to their wives and make the relationship work. These are the signs I look for when I start working with a couple that is interested in affair recovery.

1. He has cut off the affair entirely.

If he's not willing to give her up, you cannot trust him, but if he's willing to give her up – and prove to you that he has given her up – you should take this as a very good sign.

I know, you are thinking, "How will I know? I didn't even know he was cheating!"

In your gut, you do know. Do you feel deep inside that it is over, but your brain sometimes sends you into a frenzy saying, "Don't trust, don't trust!"? Your gut is probably right, but your brain is trying to protect you from getting hurt again. Trust your gut feeling.

You are probably already doing what most women do: checking his phone while he is in the bathroom, breaking into his email and Facebook accounts, etc. What are these things showing you? What have you found? Is his behavior different? Is he staying close to home, telling you where he is, etc.?

If he works with her, ask him to see what he can do about getting transferred to a different department, working from home instead of in the office, or even applying to a new job. It's very important that he cut off contact with her in order to reduce temptation and to allow both of you to focus on repairing your relationship. There is no room for either of you to think about her. You both need to focus on each other and your relationship right now.

If he is willing to do this, this is a very good sign. If he continues to show signs that he has given her up completely, take each day that he stays away from her as yet another positive sign that he truly wants to recommit to you.

2. He says he is sorry and that he won't do it again.
This might sound overly simple, but you might be amazed at how many men never apologize for going outside the marriage and never promise to remain faithful in the future.

If your man sincerely wants to repair the relationship, he will do this – and he will probably do it naturally and with great emotion.

When he apologizes and promises to remain faithful to you, look him in the eye and say:

"I need you to keep this promise – not just to me, but to yourself. If I trust you and give you a chance, you need to promise me that you will be honest with me if you are not happy instead of going outside of our relationship. Cheating is not an option."

It might help him understand your perspective more if you tell him something like the following:

"I haven't always been perfectly happy with our relationship, but I chose to deal with my dissatisfaction instead of cheating. I expect the same respect from you. If you are so unhappy, then you need to just leave, not cheat. Don't ever do this to me again."

If he responds with humility and more promises to be honest with what he needs instead of cheating, and if he takes responsibility for his infidelity, these are good signs that the two of you can work this out if you choose to do so.

However, it needs to be more than, "I'm sorry." The apology needs to ring with true regret and remorse. He must be sorry that he *hurt you*. Not that he was caught, not because you think he is a "bad guy." That kind of sorry is him feeling sorry for him*self*. (Emphasis on *self*). He needs to acknowledge that he hurt you and that he will not hurt you again.

Hopefully, he does understand that he hurt himself. I can't imagine growing up assuming that you would cheat on your wife. I hope he does indeed truly feel disappointed in himself. But, for the purposes of winning you back, he needs to be sorry for hurting *you*.

3. He offers to be transparent to prove to you (through actions) that he won't do it again.

You've heard the saying "actions speak louder than words," right? This adage applies to affair recovery extremely well.

You will want to watch his actions much more closely than his words. Many men will say they are sorry, that they have cut off the relationship with the affair partner, and that they want to make the marriage work. However, the truly committed men are willing to be completely transparent in order to *prove* to you that they are 100% committed to you.

You should look for signs like:

- He offers his phone to you so you can check his text messages at any time.
- He gives you access to his email accounts.
- He tells you if he was contacted by his affair partner and exactly what he said and did. (And he looks terrified that he will be in trouble, even though *he* didn't initiate with *her*. However, he has chosen to be honest with you in order to regain your trust.)
- He confides in you what he needs from you in the relationship, openly and vulnerably asking for *you* to be the *one person* who meets his needs.
- He tells you where he is going, who he will be with, and when he will be home – and he actually follows through. This shows that he understands how much the lies and betrayal hurt your trust in him and that you need to know where he is in order to trust again.

If he is transparent with you in these ways, these are very good signs that he is willing to make the relationship work.

4. He stays close to you and home.

If your husband realizes that his decision to go outside the marriage almost cost him the love of his life, he will want to be home with you as much as possible. He will cancel usual outings with the guys, will stop working late, and will make time to be with you. He will also prioritize doing things he believes make you happy and secure.

Now, I'm not going to say he will totally get what you need, because a lot of men are clueless about what women want from their partners. For example, he might initiate sex every night because having sex with you makes *him* feel closer to you and makes *him* feel secure, and he might project that onto you, thinking it also makes you feel close to him and secure. You might not be ready for sex with him again for a long time, and you might feel angry and think he's pushing you in an unreasonable way. Or he might be right, and making love might indeed make you feel closer.

I don't know how you feel about having sex right now; I've worked with women who had polar opposite reactions. But please listen to the point I'm making, which is that it's important to look at the *intentions* behind his actions. If he's sticking around at home and driving you crazy because he's always trying to make conversation, take it as a sign that he thinks talking with you is the solution, and he is trying to get close to you. If he spends a lot of time at home, or seems reluctant to do anything without you, these are all signs that he is trying to make things right with you.

5. He takes the lead in repairing the relationship.

Is he nice to you? Does he treat you like he did something wrong to you? If you say you want counseling, does he look up and book an appointment with a counselor?

A man who wants to win you back will work hard to show you that he loves you and wants to make things right. He will do things like:

21

- Answer your questions about the affair. (Although you should be careful with this. For example, it's best not to ask for too many details about the sexual experiences he had with his affair partner – it might damage your relationship forever.)
- End relationships with men who are bad influences on him – the "friends" who didn't help him turn towards his marriage.
- Invest extra time in the kids.
- Help you around the house or do household projects he thinks you'd appreciate.
- Hold you when you are sad and let you cry it out.
- Patiently and remorsefully accept your wrath when you get angry about the affair.
- Offer to let you sleep in or otherwise pamper yourself.
- Buy you gifts, or bring you flowers or get you a gift certificate for a massage, if those are things he knows you like.
- Ask you what you need in order to forgive him or feel secure.

If your husband is taking action to repair the relationship (and he will probably do so imperfectly, because he is human after all), you can feel pretty sure that he is sincere about recommitting to you. All of the signs listed here are great signs that he really wants to make the relationship work.

Conclusion: You should take him back if......
If your husband is showing the signs I've listed above, he probably understands that your life has been

horribly changed and that he is going to have to work hard to win you back. It sounds like he "gets" that you are sad and angry for a reason and aren't just going to "get over it" any time soon. He is taking responsibility for the affair, and he loves you enough to do the work to repair the relationship.

This is the sort of man you should consider trusting.

However, there are men that are not worth the time of day. Read on to learn what seven signs indicate that a man is untrustworthy and should not be trusted.

7 Signs He is Going to Cheat Again
(And You Will Be Hurt Again)

I've described the kind of husband who is truly sorry for cheating and who is ready to recommit to his wife.

Unfortunately, some unfaithful husbands really do fit that popular saying: "Once a cheater, always a cheater." Although I don't have a crystal ball, the following are signs that your husband is not going to remain committed to you and will probably cheat on you again.

1. He won't give up his affair partner.
This is the biggest warning sign of all. A husband who can't (or won't) give up his affair partner is not committed to you and only you. You might encounter this problem in any of the following ways:

He says he can handle being in touch with her as "just friends."
If he says he wants to "just stay friends" with her, tell him to get out. His affair partner is toxic to your marriage, and it is pretty much impossible for a man and woman who have had an affair to scale back the attraction suddenly to an acceptable level. He might genuinely care about her, and he may feel like her friendship is important to him, but the truth is that this woman is DANGER. If he doesn't recognize this (or won't admit his weakness), he is a fool playing with fire. Chances are he will succumb to temptation at some point in the future.

A rare exception to this may be a co-worker situation where he had sex with her just for the sex – with no emotional connection. You will want to take the quiz in the next chapter to determine what type of affair he had so you know if it was an affair born out of opportunity and is not emotionally threatening to the marriage.

If he needs to be in contact with her for his job, you may need to work something out where he manages to never be alone with her or work late with her. If possible, it's best if he finds a new job. He might be able to be in contact with her for work reasons only while he's looking for a new position or job.

He tells you the affair is over...and then you find out he has been in contact with her.

Of course, I'm not talking about some crazy woman who is stalking him, and he's being a perfect gentleman telling her to go away and that he's committed to you. I'm referring to you finding out that he is doing one or more of the following:

- Communicating with her, especially if it's about personal things like your marriage.
- Love letters/text messages/emails/voicemails about how much he misses her or wishes they could still be together.
- Meeting up with her, even if it's just in public for coffee (but especially if they have met up alone and had sex again).

Basically, if he's not ready to give her up yet, he's not ready to commit to you and only you.

It is important for you to understand that many men do get emotionally involved with their affair partners, and it is typically difficult for men to let go of that relationship. However, a man who wants to make his marriage work will get support from a therapist (individually, so he doesn't hurt you more), clergy, or respected friend so he can deal with the pain of the loss without hurting you or returning to her.

2. He wants you to believe him instantly without doing the work to rebuild your trust.

Your husband has just broken your heart. He has embarrassed you, made you feel like a fool for trusting him. He has disrupted the applecart that was your secure married life, spilling the many pieces of your life all over the place.

You have the right to be furious. Devastated. Distrustful. Insecure. In need of comfort and assurance.

If your husband is impatient with your need to rage, vent, cry, question, or be reassured, there's something wrong. These are signs that he doesn't get how much he hurt you, which means there is a high chance that he will betray you again.

It also is a sign that he may have an entitlement problem and think his affair was not that big of a deal. If he wants you to "just get over it" and is more concerned with you forgiving him and moving on than helping you heal, he probably is not in touch with how damaging his actions were to the relationship.

A man like this is likely to reoffend. Don't trust him until he has proven that he "gets" how much he hurt you and he is willing to do the work to win back your trust.

3. He gets angry when you ask where he is or want to look at his phone.

This is a sign that he has something to hide or doesn't get that he has to earn your trust back. A man who has cheated on you and wants to prove his innocence should humbly and willingly hand you his phone anytime you want to look at it. He should be glad to provide you with the passwords to his email accounts or Facebook account as well.

The only time a man who is trying to repair a relationship after infidelity might justifiably get angry when you ask for his phone is if you do it repeatedly, in a shaming or vindictive way. If you are a jerk to him every time you ask for it, and he has eaten humble pie repeatedly and never has had anything suspicious on his phone, then you have simply pushed him too far. If this is the case, you probably need to think through whether you are capable of forgiving him and moving on. Your inability to forgive might be the death knell for the relationship, not his inability to recommit to you.

As a general rule, men who humbly allow you to read their personal emails and text messages are trying to make the relationship work. Men who angrily rebuff your requests for access to those communication records are usually hiding something or are unrepentant.

4. He makes you take the lead.

If you're the one pushing for him to take actions that will repair the relationship, he's probably not serious about trying to make things work.

Bad signs are:

- He makes you inquire about couples counseling (instead of him doing the legwork).
- He is resistant when you suggest seeing a minister.
- You are the one downloading a book to read on relationship repair (not him).

Recovering from an affair takes work – a lot of work. It is difficult to trust someone who has broken your heart. If he's not willing to do the work, chances are the relationship will just deteriorate further, and he will cheat again. Look for signs that he is willing to work at the relationship, even without your prompting.

5. He blames you for the affair.

If the first words out of his mouth are not, "I'm so sorry – I've made the worst choices of my entire life," but rather, "It's your fault. You made me do it," then you're in trouble. Men who blame their partners for their own poor decisions are usually incapable of taking responsibility for those poor choices. This type of man will most likely make the same poor decisions again.

This is different from when you ask him why he cheated and he answers you in a calm way, explaining he felt deprived because you rarely had sex or that he was starving for attention because you criticized him too much. I'm not talking about him trying to give you a reason so you will understand why he was vulnerable (and what you can do to help him be strong and faithful). I'm talking about him intentionally blaming you for the affair.

I say this because many affairs are born out of unmet needs in relationships. Many men go outside of the marriage to get needs met because they are either too afraid to ask you to meet their needs (out of fear of conflict or that you will not respect them) or don't believe you are capable of meeting those needs.

If you decide to stick it out, you will probably find out he was unhappy in some way or had an emotional need that he did not know how to get met. Perhaps he feels he is unattractive and therefore needed more affirmation. Maybe you only had sex once a month, and the thought that he would feel sexually deprived for his entire life saddened him, especially since he had trusted you to keep him sexually satisfied. You may need to listen to what he needs, and then decide if you can meet those needs or not.

However, all of this is very different from a man accusing you of "making" him cheat or blaming his affair on you. If he won't take responsibility and puts the blame on you, you should take this as a sign that he will likely cheat again in the future and is unable to truly repair the relationship.

6. You are not married.
There wasn't a time of clarity when he knew you were "the one" and stood up in front of the world and

declared that he loved you more than anyone else. And now he has cheated on you.

I hate to say this to you, but he just might not be that into you. Living together isn't married. Married is married.

Women in my office are often confused as to why their man won't marry them. The answer is simple. A man will live with, be in a relationship with, and have sex with a woman that isn't "the one". Often a man will move in with a girl because it is the "next step," and he doesn't want to rock the boat. He figures it will be cozy, that he'll get more sex. It isn't that he hates you. He doesn't. You just aren't "the one."

My advice to you is to move on. You hit a rough patch in the relationship, and he partnered with someone else. Marriage and life are tough. You might experience job loss, pregnancy, a special needs child and/or the death of a parent. At these times, you are going to your unvarnished self and you aren't going to be the perfect partner. You need someone whom you can trust to have confidence in you and the relationship, and he certainly is not it. Save yourself from more heartache and find someone who thinks you are "the one."

7. He is a sex addict.
Has he had sex with multiple women? Has he been repeatedly unfaithful to you? Have you noticed an increase in demand, like he has to have sex more and more to be satisfied? Has it become difficult to get him off (which is a sign of tolerance, due to having a lot of sex)?

If you suspect your husband is addicted to sex and is unable to be satisfied with the amount of sexual engagement you find enjoyable, you may be dealing with a sex addict.

Of course, mismatched libido is common. I see a lot of couples where one partner wants more sex than the other. It's tough to find a partner who wants exactly the same amount of sexual intimacy that you do, and men tend to want sex more often than women (hence the stereotypes and jokes). However, if you've wondered if your husband is addicted to sex, you may want to learn more about this.

There are many online quizzes available that will help you determine if your husband has a problem with sexual addiction.

Here are two well-known online quizzes:

IITAP International Institute for Trauma & Addiction Professionals:

http://www.sexhelp.com/am-i-a-sex-addict/sex-addiction-test

Sex Addicts Anonymous
https://saa-recovery.org/IsSAAForYou/SelfAssessment/

If you decide that your husband is probably a sex addict, ask him to get help from a skilled therapist. In the meantime, protect yourself from heartbreak by pulling away and preparing yourself for the possibility that he may be a repeat offender.

Conclusion: You Should Cut Your Losses and Move On If...

So, you are reading this book because you aren't sure if you should stay or go. I've taken you through the signs that look like he's cheating but isn't, signs that he is a good man who made a bad decision, and signs that he is probably going to do this again.

I know it's hard to let go, and I know the thought of divorce is overwhelming. However, if he is displaying the "cheat again" signs, he's probably just going to hurt you again. It might be hard in the short term to break off the relationship, but by this, you will free yourself to heal and to find a man who truly loves and values you.

Diagnosing Your Situation
(What Exactly Are You Dealing With?)

While I like to give couples hope that they can indeed survive an affair, I also feel that it's important that they address the affair straightforwardly, with an open mind. In my experience, certain types of affairs are easier or more difficult to recover from. Learning what type of an affair your husband had acts as a good predictor of the likelihood or unlikelihood of future indiscretions.

You will want to determine what type of affair your husband had, and then think through what it will take to work through the issues at hand. Knowing the type of affair can also help you determine if you want to stick it out or if you would be better off giving up on the marriage and moving on.

Diagnostic Quiz: What Type of Affair Did Your Husband Have?

The following is a quiz I ask husbands to take to determine what type of affair they have had. Take this quiz as if you are your husband, trying to answer it as he would. Better yet, have your husband take the quiz and discuss his answers together, if you are at a point in recovery where you can discuss the affair together in a constructive manner.

Diagnostic Quiz: Types of Affairs

To determine what type of affair you had, answer yes or no to the following questions. Then compare your answers to those listed in the different affair types listed below. Your answers may point to more than one affair type. Your affair type will be the one where you answer the most questions in relation to that type.

1. Do you and your wife fight a lot? *no*
2. Was it easy for you to end the affair? *no*
3. Are you tempted to go back to your affair partner? *he did*
4. Have you talked to your wife about your needs and wants in the relationship, yet you still feel she is unwilling to help you meet them? *no*
5. Do you feel emotionally distant from your wife and kids? *?*
6. Do you think you should be able to have everything you want in life? *?*
7. Was your affair a one-night stand? *no*
8. Do you desire to end your marriage? *no*
9. Do you avoid talking to your partner about problems that may lead to disagreements? *yes*
10. Do you feel guilty about having an affair? *I do*
11. Are you generally a risk taker? *no*
12. Do you lie to avoid unpleasant things, not just in your marriage, but in different parts of your life? *yes*
13. Have you cut most or all of the emotional ties to your marriage? *no*
14. Has your spouse also had an affair? *no*
15. Have you made a lot of personal sacrifices to try to make your marriage work? *yes*
16. Was your affair unplanned and spontaneous? *no*

17. Do you try to be emotionally engaged and actively involved with your wife and children? *yes*
18. Was this a short-term affair (less than 6 months)? *borderline — would never have ended*
19. Do you feel ambivalent about ending your marriage, even if you have decided that you want to do so?
20. Did your affair happen due to unusual events, such as travel, drugs, or alcohol, which normally isn't an issue in your relationship? *no*
21. Is your biggest fear that of being discovered? *IDK*
22. Was your affair partner a friend before you started cheating with that person? *yes*

Types of Affairs

Now tally up his answers (or your answers, answering as if you were him) and determine what type of affair your husband had.

The Conflict Avoidance Affair:

If you answered NO to question 1 and YES to questions 2, 9, 10, and 18, you fit this type.

You do everything possible to avoid fighting with your wife. You don't want to hurt her feelings and don't want to get into conflict with her.

You fear that your wife will abandon you or otherwise hurt you if you express or admit your needs. You may even struggle with disagreeing with your wife and feel like you are constantly making concessions to keep the peace.

Because of this, you don't tell your wife what you need and want for fear of upsetting her. You had an affair to

35

try to get your needs met that you feared your wife would not meet. You tend to have short-term affairs and are not emotionally attached to your affair partner because your primary motivation for the affair is to get specific needs met and to avoid conflict with your wife.

To repair your marriage, you will have to confront your fear of conflict and learn how to express your needs clearly and openly. You may also need to learn to trust that other people are capable of hearing what you need and meeting those needs.

Perhaps you doubt your wife is capable of change, and you have given up on trying to get your needs met inside the marriage. You may need an infusion of hope and trust, combined with a commitment to being open with your wife about your needs or dissatisfaction. You may need help finding solutions.

The Intimacy Avoidance Affair:
If you answered YES to questions 1, 2, 5, 14, and 18, you fit this type.

You are afraid to get close to your wife. You find yourself fighting with your wife on a regular basis to avoid getting close to her and revealing your emotional vulnerability. You are also not emotionally invested in your affair partner and you can easily end the affair. Your affair served as a way to stay emotionally distant from your wife.

If you want to repair your marriage, you will need to learn how to develop an intimate relationship with your wife. This requires vulnerability and allowing yourself to be "seen" and loved as you are. You can work on this in therapy individually and/or with your wife.

The Affair Born Out of Unmet Emotional Needs:

If you answered NO to question 10 and YES to questions 4, 15, 17, and 22, you fit this type.

There is something in your marriage that makes you unhappy. You feel you need more than your wife is giving. You have discussed your needs with your wife, and she has not made changes necessary to help fulfill your needs. You feel your affair is justified because of this. However, you are not ready to give up on the marriage.

This is the most common reason that good men make the bad decision to have an affair. I encourage you to seek couples counseling after the initial turmoil has died down. You have an excellent chance of saving your marriage – if your wife stays and you learn how to express your needs to her in a way that helps her understand how important these issues are to you.

The Split Selves Affair:

If you answered NO to question 2 and YES to questions 3, 6, 15, and 17, you fit this type.

You feel devoted to your marriage and try to do everything right. You have made many sacrifices to make your marriage work, and now you are feeling the burden of subjugating your own needs for the needs of your family.

You are very involved with household activities and are probably known as an excellent parent and partner. However, you feel like the relationship has been unfair. Under this weight, you strayed from the marriage to get your needs met.

Most likely you feel very loving towards your affair partner and may be having a tough time breaking ties with her. You want both a happy marriage and an affair partner because you now love both people.

This is also a main reason couples find themselves in my office. There is an excellent chance you will have the marriage you want because you are capable of emotionally investing in a relationship.

 ## The Entitlement Affair:
If you answered NO to questions 10 and 17 and YES to questions 5, 6, 11, and 12, you fit this type.

You feel like you deserve to have everything you want. You have always been treated as special and you work hard to get what you believe you deserve. Very few people have ever said no to you. Your parents gave you everything you wanted as a child. You feel little guilt about the affair you had.

Please take the Sexual Addiction survey to see if this is part of your struggle. Please do NOT try to recover your marriage if you are only going to cheat again! Instead, get help from a therapist (individually) to work through your issues, whether it be with sexual addiction or with feeling like you should be able to have everything your way.

The Opportunistic/One Night Stand Affair:
If you answered YES to questions 7, 10, 16, 20, and 21, you fit this type.

These are unplanned, spontaneous affairs. Often people who have these types of affairs did not plan to do so. There is oftentimes no real issue in the marriage leading to the affair. In many cases, they involve a stranger. Generally, these are isolated incidents. Travels, such as business trips, or alcohol or drugs may contribute to the affair.

You probably feel a lot of guilt over this and fear being discovered. Please take the Sexual Addiction survey to see if this is contributing to your struggle.

The Exit Strategy Affair:
If you answered NO to question 10 and YES to questions 5, 8, 13, and 19, you fit this type.

You are ready to end the marriage and are using an affair as a launching board to accomplish your goal. You may or may not have started the affair intentionally as a way to get out of your marriage, but you subconsciously hope she will find out you are cheating and dump you so you don't have to be the bad guy who divorced her. Ironically, you may prefer to be the bad guy who was caught cheating!

If you feel this way, it is time to meet with an individual therapist or minister to determine if this is true and, if so, how you can separate from your wife.

Conclusion: Respond appropriately to the root of the problem.

I hope you were able to identify an affair type (or two – affairs don't always neatly fit into one category) and now feel like you have a better idea as to how you should proceed. You probably noticed that therapy is a common recommendation. This is because it can be very difficult for couples to work through the hurt feelings and causes of an affair without support from an unbiased third person who will know how to guide you through the process.

Conclusion:
Should You Stay or Should You Go?

I know you are in the middle of probably the most painful decision of your life. You've been betrayed by the one person you trusted to always be in your corner, and you're trying to decide if it's worth it to keep trying or if you'd be better off if you moved on.

I hope you've gleaned some helpful information from this book. My final advice is this: Please take your time as you make this very important decision. Get advice from a relationship expert, and give yourself some time to get over the initial shock before you burn any bridges. Many couples make it through affairs and come out stronger and closer than before.

Remember, before you even consider taking him back, you need to determine the following:

- If he is truly remorseful (not just "sorry").
- If he is willing to take responsibility for the poor decisions he made.
- If he understands how much he hurt you and is willing to help you heal.
- If he is sincerely and wholeheartedly recommitting himself to you.
- If he is willing to do the work to earn back your trust.

It is my hope that you will find the best solution for your situation. Whatever happens, I wish you love and happiness.

Wishing you well,

Caroline Madden
Marriage Therapist

Resources

It is challenging for a couple to recover from an affair without professional help. Each partner can get stuck in a phase that, without guidance, will doom the relationship. But if you are taking the self-help approach, these are the books to read together as a couple:

After the Affair, Updated Second Edition: Healing the Pain and Rebuilding Trust When a Partner Has Been Unfaithful by Janis A. Spring

The Sex-Starved Marriage: Boosting Your Marriage Libido: A Couple's Guide by Michele Weiner Davis

Wanting Sex Again: How to Rediscover Your Desire and Heal a Sexless Marriage by Laura Watson

For other book recommendations please visit my therapist website: www.CounselingWithCaroline.com.

Peer Resource

Infidelity Counseling Network
www.infidelitycounselingnetwork.org

Offers free, confidential, one-to-one telephone peer support by trained peer counselors, all of whom are women who have survived infidelity whether they are married, divorced, separated, or single. They work with each client toward her personal recovery from infidelity, for as long as she wants or needs, regardless of whether her relationship ends or mends.

About the Author:

Caroline Madden, MFT is a Los Angeles-based pro-marriage therapist and author of several relationship books. She specializes in Affair Recovery. On a personal note, she is the mother of two young boys. She knows first hand how life altering becoming a mother can be. Ms. Madden has been in the same loving relationship for over 15 years and understands that even the best relationships take work. For more information about her, please visit her author website: www.CarolineMadden.com.

More Books By Caroline Madden, MFT:

How to Go From Soul Mates to Roommates in 10 Easy Steps

When Your Spouse Loses A Parent: What to Say & What to Do

After a Good Man Cheats: How to Rebuild Trust & Intimacy with Your Wife

Would you like a FREE eBook?

As thanks for purchasing this book, my publisher would like to send you a free eBook. Visit their website to pre-order your free eBook:

http://trainofthoughtpress.com/get-a-book-for-free/

Please consider leaving this book a positive review on Amazon.

I hope that you found *Fool Me Once: Should I Take Back My Cheating Husband?* useful.

If you did, please consider giving it a **positive review** on Amazon. Thank you in advance.

All my best,
Caroline Madden, MFT

Made in the USA
San Bernardino, CA
21 April 2017